IF I ONLY KNEW

NELLY SACHS
If I Only Knew

Selected, translated and introduced by
Jean Boase-Beier

Edited by Philip Wilson

Arc Publications
2023

Published by Arc Publications,
Nanholme Mill, Shaw Wood Road
Todmorden OL14 6DA, UK
www.arcpublications.co.uk

978 1911469-39 1

Design by Tony Ward
Cover photograph by Tony Ward
Printed in Great Britain by TJ Books Ltd, Padstow, Cornwall

Acknowledgements

Arc Publications is grateful to the above named publisher for granting rights to reproduce these poems in the original German and in translation.

The translator, Jean Boase-Beier, would like to thank Philip Wilson for careful reading and pertinent questions and also Dieter Beier for helping prepare and check the manuscript.

GOETHE INSTITUT

The translation of this work was supported by a grant from the Goethe-Institut

Arc Chapbook Series
Series Editor: Tony Ward

CONTENTS

PUBLISHERS' NOTE

Arc's contractual agreement with Suhrkamp Verlag specifies that the poems and their translations should not be preceded by an introductory essay, although it does allow for an Afterword.

The reader may, therefore, find it helpful to read Jean Boase-Beier's Afterword before reading the poems themselves.

'WENN ICH NUR WÜSSTE...'

Wenn ich nur wüßte,
Worauf dein letzter Blick ruhte.
War es ein Stein, der schon viele letzte Blicke
Getrunken hatte, bis sie in Blindheit
Auf den Blinden fielen?

Oder war es Erde,
Genug, um einen Schuh zu füllen,
Und schon schwarz geworden
Von soviel Abschied
Und von soviel Tod bereiten?

Oder war es dein letzter Weg,
Der dir das Lebewohl von allen Wegen brachte
Die du gegangen warst?

Eine Wasserlache, ein Stück spiegelndes Metall,
Vielleicht die Gürtelschnalle deines Feindes,
Oder irgend ein anderer, kleiner Wahrsager
Des Himmels?

Oder sandte dir diese Erde,
Die keinen ungeliebt von hinnen gehen läßt
Ein Vogelzeichen durch die Luft,
Erinnernd deine Seele, daß sie zuckte
In ihrem qualverbrannten Leib?

'IF I ONLY KNEW...'

One of Sachs' earlier post-war poems, which appeared in her first book, In den Wohnungen des Todes (In the Houses of Death, 1947), *published when she was 56. It was written in 1943 or 1944, as part of a small group of poems entitled 'Prayers for the dead bridegroom'. There is some evidence (and much speculation in Sachs criticism) that these poems were inspired by a man she had loved as a young woman in Berlin, and who had, perhaps, either in reality or in Sachs' imagination, later been killed by the Nazis. Whether real or imaginary, the person addressed appears to be facing death, possibly by execution.*

If I only knew
What your final glance rested upon.
Was it a stone, that had drunk many,
Many final glances, until, gone blind,
They fell on the blind man?

Or was it earth,
Enough to fill a shoe,
And turned completely black
From all this leave-taking
From all this doing to death?

Or was it your final path
That brought you farewell to all paths
You had ever walked?

A puddle, a piece of shining metal
Perhaps the buckle of your enemy's belt,
Or some other small foreteller
Of heaven?

Or did this earth
That lets no single one depart unloved
Send you a bird-sign through the air,
To call back your soul, so it quivered
In its body ravaged by fire?

IHR ZUSCHAUENDEN

Unter deren Blicken getötet wurde.
Wie man auch einen Blick im Rücken fühlt,
So fühlt ihr an euerm Leibe
Die Blicke der Toten.

Wieviel brechende Augen werden euch ansehn
Wenn ihr aus den Verstecken ein Veilchen pflückt?
Wieviel flehend erhobene Hände
In dem märtyrerhaft geschlungenen Gezweige
Der alten Eichen?
Wieviel Erinnerung wächst im Blute
Der Abendsonne?

O die ungesungenen Wiegenlieder
In der Turteltaube Nachtruf –
Manch einer hätte Sterne herunterholen können,
Nun muß es der alte Brunnen für ihn tun!

Ihr Zuschauenden,
Die ihr keine Mörderhand erhobt,
Aber die ihr den Staub nicht von eurer Sehnsucht
Schütteltet,
Die ihr stehenbliebt, dort, wo er zu Licht
Verwandelt wird.

YOU BYSTANDERS

Sachs often addresses specific groups of people who were involved in the Holocaust, as though, living in exile in Sweden, she is trying to form a picture of what happened. Here she addresses one group she held partly responsible for the terrors und upheavals she had suffered, and for the fate of her people. In doing so, she tries to imagine what they must have been thinking at the time, and what the future will hold for them. The old well in the third stanza is probably a reference to the poem of that title by Hans Carossa, a German poet who rejected Nazism but also accommodated to it.

Under whose gaze murder was done.
Just as we feel an eye-gaze from behind,
So you feel in your bodies
The gaze of the dead.

How many breaking eyes will stare at you
When you pick a violet from its cover?
How many pleading lifted hands
In the martyred knotted branches
Of old oaks?
How much memory grows in the blood
Of the evening sun?

Oh, the unsung lullabies
In the night-call of a turtle dove –
One of them might have drawn down the stars
But now the old well must do it for them.

You bystanders,
You who raised no hand to kill,
But who let the dust remain on your longing,
Not shaken off,
You who stood still there, where it is changed
Into light.

CHOR DER TRÖSTER

Gärtner sind wir, blumenlos gewordene
Kein Heilkraut lässt sich pflanzen
Von Gestern nach Morgen.
Der Salbei hat abgeblüht in den Wiegen –
Rosmarin seinen Duft im Angesicht der neuen
  Toten verloren –
Selbst der Wermut war bitter nur für gestern.
Die Blüten des Trostes sind zu kurz entsprossen
Reichen nicht für die Qual einer Kinderträne.

Neuer Same wird vielleicht
Im Herzen eines nächtlichen Sängers gezogen.
Wer von uns darf trösten?
In der Tiefe des Hohlwegs
Zwischen Gestern und Morgen
Steht der Cherub
Mahlt mit seinen Flügeln die Blitze der Trauer
Seine Hände aber halten die Felsen auseinander
Von Gestern und Morgen
Wie die Ränder einer Wunde
Die offenbleiben soll
Die noch nicht heilen darf.

Nicht einschlafen lassen die Blitze der Trauer
Das Feld des Vergessens.

Wer von uns darf trösten?
Gärtner sind wir, blumenlos gewordene
Und stehn auf einem Stern, der strahlt
Und weinen.

CHORUS OF COMFORTERS

Another poem from Sachs' 1947 collection, one of a sub-section of 'Choruses'. These choruses provide imagined responses to some of Sachs' questions about the causes and effects of the Holocaust, and are spoken by different groups, some animate (wanderers, the dead), some inanimate (stars, stones). Here she focusses especially on the aftermath, and the role of those, including herself, who were not directly involved.

We are gardeners, become flowerless
There is no healing herb we can plant
Between yesterday and tomorrow.
Sage in the cradles has dropped its flowers –
Rosemary lost its scent in the face
  of the recent dead –
Even wormwood only bitter for yesterday.
The blossoms of comfort have come up too short
Not enough for the agony of a child's tears.

Perhaps new seeds might be grown
In the heart of a singer at night.
Which of us dares comfort?
In the depths of the hollow path
Between yesterday and tomorrow
There stands a cherub
Grinding with his wings the light-flares of grief
But his hands hold apart the cliffs
Of yesterday and tomorrow
Like the edges of a wound
That must remain unclosed
That must not heal.

The light-flares of grief do not let
The field of forgetting fall asleep.

Which of us dares comfort?
We are gardeners, become flowerless
We stand upon a star that blazes
And weep.

'WENN WIE RAUCH...'

Wenn wie Rauch der Schlaf einzieht in den Leib,
und wie ein erloschenes Gestirn, das anderswo entzündet wird,
der Mensch zu Grunde fährt,
steht der Streit still,
abgetriebene Mähre, die den Alpdruck ihres Reiters
abgeworfen hat.
Aus ihrem heimlichen Takt entlassen
sind die Schritte,
die wie Brunnenschwengel an das Rätsel der Erde klopften.
Alle künstlichen Tode sind in ihre blutverwirrten Nester
heimgekehrt.

Wenn wie Rauch der Schlaf einzieht in den Leib,
atmet das Kind gestillt, mit der Mondtrompete im Arm.
Die Träne verschläft ihre Sehnsucht zu fließen,
aber die Liebe ist alle Umwege zu Ende gegangen
und ruht in ihrem Beginn.
Jetzt ist die Zeit für das Kalb seine neue Zunge
am Leib der Mutter zu proben,
der falsche Schlüssel schließt nicht
und das Messer rostet hinein
bis in die blasse Heide der Morgendämmerung
die aus der Vergessenheit erblüht im furchtbaren Frührot.

'WHEN LIKE SMOKE...'

A poem from Sachs' 1949 collection Sternverdunkelung (Darkening of the Stars)*. This was a time, just a few years after the war, when there was little acknowledgement of guilt in Germany, Sachs' homeland. There was instead a great desire to forget what had happened, not shared by philosophers like Theodor Adorno or Karl Jaspers, and certainly not shared by Sachs, who protested against it in many of her poems.*

When like smoke sleep enters the body,
and like a quenched star that is lighted elsewhere
a human goes to ground,
then conflict stills,
a worn-out mare that has thrown off the incubus
that rode it.
Those steps are freed
from their secret beat
that drummed like well-handles on the riddle of the earth.
Engineered deaths have all gone home to their blood-disordered nests.

When like smoke sleep enters the body,
the quieted child breathes calm, the moon's trumpet in her arm.
Tears, drowsing, fail to well their longing,
but love has gone the long way round to its end
and rests in its beginning.
Now is the time for a calf to try out its new tongue
on its mother's body,
the wrong key does not lock
and the knife rusts into
the pale heathland of morning-light
that blossoms out of oblivion in a red and deadly dawn.

Wenn wie Rauch der Schlaf auszieht aus dem Leib,
und der Mensch geheimnisgesättigt
die abgetriebene Mähre des Streites
aus dem Stalle treibt,
beginnt die feuerschnaubende Verbindung aufs neue
und der Tod erwacht in jeder Maienknospe
und das Kind küßt einen Stein
in der Sternverdunkelung.

When like smoke sleep leaves the body,
and sated with mystery a human
drives the worn-out mare of conflict
out of its stable,
then the fire-snorting union starts up again
and death awakes in every bud of May
the child kisses a stone
in the darkening of the stars.

'WARUM DIE SCHWARZE ANTWORT DES HASSES...'

Warum die schwarze Antwort des Hasses
auf dein Dasein, Israel?

Fremdling du,
einen Stern von weiterher
als die anderen.
Verkauft an diese Erde
damit Einsamkeit fort sich erbe.

Deine Herkunft verwachsen mit Unkraut –
deine Sterne vertauscht
gegen alles was Motten und Würmern gehört,
und doch von den Traumsandufern der Zeit
wie Mondwasser fortgeholt in die Ferne.

Im Chore der anderen
hast du gesungen
einen Ton höher
oder einen Ton tiefer –

der Abendsonne hast du dich ins Blut geworfen
wie ein Schmerz den anderen sucht.
Lang ist dein Schatten
und es ist späte Zeit für dich geworden
Israel!

Wie weit dein Weg von der Segnung
den Äon der Tränen entlang
bis zu der Wegbiegung
da du in Asche gefallen,

'WHY THE BLACK ANSWER OF HATE...'

Another poem from Sachs' collection of 1949, published one year after the founding of the state of Israel. There was still little mention of the Jews, or the hatred of the Jews that drove the Holocaust, in Germany, and Sachs is here addressing the Jews as a people, rather than their newly-founded country, and asking the age-old question: why?

Why the black answer of hate
to your existence, Israel?

You, a stranger,
from a star one further off
than the others.
Sold to this earth
So loneliness can be passed on.

Your origins grown through with weeds
your stars exchanged
for all that belongs to moths and worms,
and yet from the dreaming sandbanks of time
drawn away like moon-water into distant lands.

In the chorus of the others
you have sung
a higher note
or a lower note –

thrown yourself into the blood of the evening sun
as one pain seeks another.
Your shadow is long
and the time has grown late for you
Israel!

How far was your path from blessing
along the aeons of tears
up to the bend
where you fell to ash,

dein Feind mit dem Rauch
deines verbrannten Leibes
deine Todverlassenheit
an die Stirn des Himmels schrieb!

O solcher Tod!
Wo alle helfenden Engel
mit blutenden Schwingen
zerrissen im Stacheldraht
der Zeit hingen!

Warum die schwarze Antwort des Hasses
auf dein Dasein
Israel?

and your enemy wrote
in the smoke of your burnt body
your abandonment to death
upon the forehead of heaven!

Such a death!
Where all the assisting angels
with bleeding wings
hung torn on the barbed wire
of time!

Why the black answer of hate
to your existence
Israel?

'MIT WILDHONIG...'

Mit Wildhonig
die Hinterbliebenen
nährten
in frühen Gräbern
einbalsamierten Schlaf
und ausgewanderte Pulse
gossen Dattelwein
in die Bienenwabe
der Geheimnisse.

Im schwarzen Kristall der Nacht
die eingeschlossene Wespe
der ausgetanzten Zeit
im Starrkrampf lag –

Aber du,
aber du,
wie nähre ich dich?

Alle Meilensteine aus Staub
überspringt die Liebe,
wie die geköpfte Sonne
im Schmerz
nur Untergang suchend.

Mit meinem Untergang
nähre ich dich –

'WITH WILD HONEY...'

From Sachs' third collection, Niemand weiβ weiter (No-one Knows What to do Next, 1957)*, written as she continued the search begun more than ten years before to understand what it meant to be Jewish, by reading works of Jewish history and mysticism. Honey is a common symbol, in Judaism and other religions, for the divine. Those left behind to preserve the memory of their dead feature often in Sachs' poems, and here she wonders how she can best care for those preservers of memory, suggesting, as she does in other poems, that her own self-sacrifice might be necessary.*

With wild honey
those left behind
fed
in their early graves
embalmed sleep
and exiled pulses
poured date wine
into the honeycomb
of secrets.

In the black crystal of night
the captured wasp
of danced-out time
lay cramped and locked –

But you,
but you,
how do I feed you?

All those milestones of dust
love leaps over them,
like a beheaded sun
seeking only to go down
in its pain.

When I go down
I will feed you –

'IN DER FLUCHT...'

In der Flucht
welch großer Empfang
unterwegs –

Eingehüllt
in der Winde Tuch
Füße im Gebet des Sandes
der niemals Amen sagen kann
denn er muß von der Flosse in den Flügel
und weiter –

Der kranke Schmetterling
weiß bald wieder vom Meer –
Dieser Stein
mit der Inschrift der Fliege
hat sich mir in die Hand gegeben –

An Stelle von Heimat
halte ich die Verwandlungen der Welt –

'IN FLIGHT...'

By the time Sachs published her 1959 collection Flucht und Verwandlung (Flight and Metamorphosis), *from which this poem is taken, she had started to write poetry that was much sparer and more compressed. Many of the poems of this time reflect on her own displacement and that of so many others throughout the history of the Jewish people. And yet flight is not necessarily a negative thing, as one's identity persists, and perhaps being an exile even helps a writer to understand others who have been displaced.*

In flight
what a great reception
on the way –

Wrapped up
in the shawls of the winds
feet in the prayer of the sand
which can never say Amen
for it must go from fin to wing
and onwards –

The sick butterfly
will soon rediscover the sea –
This stone
with the fly's inscript
has put itself in my hand –

In place of home
I hold the transformations of world –

'DER SCHLAFWANDLER...'

Der Schlafwandler
kreisend auf seinem Stern
an der weißen Feder des Morgens
erwacht –
der Blutfleck darauf erinnerte ihn –
läßt den Mond erschrocken fallen –
die Schneebeere zerbricht
am schwarzen Achat der Nacht –
traumbesudelt –

Kein reines Weiß auf Erden –

'THE SLEEP-WALKER...'

A poem from the late 1950s, when Sachs was suffering badly from persecution anxiety. Though metaphorical poems like this can seem difficult or obscure, in fact the central idea is clear: what has happened in the past continues to have negative effects in the present. For Sachs, this applied both to her own state of mind and to society in general. News of the rise of Neo-Nazis in Germany caused her particular anguish. Sachs often used generic masculine forms, as is still common in German, but no longer common today in English. I assume she was speaking of herself in this poem, so I translate these forms as 'she / her'. Sachs' use of the verb 'erinnern' (to remind, but literally to bring inside) is idiosyncratic here, as it is in 'If I Only Knew...' (page 8). The sleep-walker is not reminded of anything; she is reminded in the sense of being brought back into her mind.

The sleep-walker
circling on her star
on the white feather of morning
awakes –
the blood-spot on it has re-minded her –
shocked she lets the moon fall –
the snowberry breaks up
on the black agate of night –
dream-stained –

No pure white on earth –

'TOD...'

Tod
Meergesang
spülend um meinen Leib
salzige Traube
durstlockende in meinem Mund –

Aufschlägst du die Saiten meiner Adern
bis sie singend springen
knospend aus den Wunden
die Musik meiner Liebe zu spielen –

Deine entfächerten Horizonte
mit der Zackenkrone aus Sterben
schon um den Hals gelegt
das Ritual des Aufbruchs
mit dem gurgelnden Laut der Atemzüge
begonnen
verließest du nach Verführerart
vor der Hochzeit das bezauberte Opfer
entkleidet schon fast bis auf den Sand
verstoßen
aus zwei Königreichen
nur noch Seufzer
zwischen Nacht und Nacht –

'DEATH...'

Another poem from the late 1950s, one of several that addresses death directly. Though she would live for more than ten years, Sachs has sometimes been described as longing for death at this time. But it would perhaps be more correct to say she accepted it, seeing death as a necessary prerequisite to union with the Divine. She also regards death, here as in many other poems and writings, as a force that helps her write, and that her writing will transcend.

Death
sea-songs
swishing round my body
salty grape
thirst-drawing in my mouth

You open up the strings of my arteries
until they spring singing
budding out of wounds
to play the music of my love –

Your fanned-out horizons
with the jagged crown of death
already round your throat
the ritual of leaving
begun
with the gurgling sounds of breath
like a seducer you would leave
the enchanted victim before the wedding
undressed almost to the sand
cast out
from two realms
now only a sigh
between night and night –

'IHR MEINE TOTEN...'

Ihr meine Toten
Eure Träume sind Waisen geworden
Nacht hat die Bilder verdeckt
Fliegend in Chiffren eure Sprache singt

Die Flüchtlingsschar der Gedanken
eure wandernde Hinterlassenschaft
bettelt an meinem Strand

Unruhig bin ich
sehr erschrocken
den Schatz zu fassen mit kleinem Leben

Selbst Inhaber von Augenblicken
Herzklopfen Abschieden
Todeswunden
wo ist mein Erbe

Salz ist mein Erbe

'YOU MY DEAD...'

Written close to the end of her life, in 1969 or 1970, this poem, given to friends and published posthumously, again addresses a particular group of people, as do so many of her poems. Here she questions her place among those who have died before her, and, clearly referring to the Jewish people, wonders whether she can speak for them.

You my dead
Your dreams have been orphaned
Night has hidden the images
Your tongue sings flying over symbols

The refugee-storm of thoughts
your wandering legacy
begs upon my shore

And I am uneasy
profoundly shocked
to grasp the prize with my tiny life

Myself the holder of moments
of heartbeats farewells
death-wounds
where is my inheritance

salt is my inheritance

AFTERWORD

When Nelly Sachs was awarded the Nobel Prize for Literature in 1966, which she received jointly with Hebrew novelist and short-story writer Shmuel Josef Agnon, she was a famous writer, at least in Germany, the country of her birth, and Sweden, where she lived.

Photographs taken at various events in her honour around this time show a tiny, delicate-looking woman with large dark eyes, thin little legs, and a huge handbag. Video footage of her Nobel speech shows her to be gracious, poised, and rather shy. Her appearance was often commented on in news reports, especially in Germany, and it seems to have had an effect on the way her poetry was perceived. At this time Germany clearly needed to see in her a poet of reconciliation, and she looked the part.

But she was a far more complex figure than these appealing images suggest. She was hard-working and determined, and since childhood her life had not been easy. By the time she was in her late thirties she had spent many years caring for her seriously ill father. Ten years later, having suffered constant harassment by the Nazi authorities because she was Jewish, she managed at the last moment to secure a passage to Sweden for herself and her mother, and then quickly adapted to their greatly reduced circumstances, supporting the two of them with her work as a translator. And all the time, in spite of suffering from periods of mental distress and breakdown, she continued to develop as a poet who spoke of the history and suffering of the Jewish people.

Born in 1891 into a wealthy Jewish family in Berlin, she had lived a rather sheltered life as a girl. Her father, Georg William Sachs, owned a large factory for latex products such as raincoats and medical instruments, and in 1887 patented an early version of the chest expander, sold as exercise equipment for men and women. Their daughter Leonie, known as Nelly, was an introverted child, fond of music and dancing, and with an interest in writing which she developed during her years at school. Shortly after leaving school, when she was 17, she fell in love with a man about whom little is known. The experience was a very unhappy one for Sachs, and it resulted in the first of several breakdowns that required treatment in hospital. She was 39 when William Sachs died of cancer, and her life, like that of all Jews in Germany, became increasingly difficult when Hitler came to power three years later, in 1933. She had had several poems published in journals and newspapers by then, but publication soon became impossible for Jews. Her early poems, often about nature and animals, are competent, but very conventional, and they seem somewhat naïve for a woman in her 30s and 40s. Indeed, Sachs often spoke rather disparagingly in later years of this early work.

Sachs and her mother, Margarete, lived in constant fear. Helped by the Swedish writer Selma Lagerlöff (author of *The Wonderful Adventures of Nils*), with whom she had been in contact for nearly 20 years, as well as by friends in Germany, the two women fled to Sweden in 1940, and began a new life in Stockholm. Sachs worked as an archivist and she learned Swedish quickly so she could translate Swedish poetry into German.

Her book *Von Welle und Granit* (Of Waves and Granite) contains translations of twentieth-century Swedish poetry, and appeared with the Aufbau Verlag in East Berlin, in 1947. Aufbau, like all publishing houses in the German Democratic Republic, was subject to strict censorship, and specialised mainly in anti-fascist writing, exile literature, and approved German and Russian classics. That same year, her first collection of original poetry, *In den Wohnungen des Todes* (In the Houses of Death) was also published by Aufbau.

Sachs states in the Foreword to *Von Welle und Granit* that her collection of translations is intended to allow German readers access to poets almost unknown in the German-speaking world. She describes the poems, many of them the work of Swedish Modernists such as Gunnar Ekelöf, Johannes Edfelt, and Harry Martinson, as based on thought rather than emotion, and her translations demonstrate a striking competence in rhythm and rhyme.

Her own poems written at this time arose as a response to news of the suffering of Jewish people in Germany. Her 1947 collection contains some of her best-known work, such as 'O die Schornsteine...' ('Oh, the chimneys...'), but many of the poems can seem a little over-emotional for today's taste, full of 'Oh's and exclamations, and rather artless repetitions. Other poems are more restrained and questioning, and three of these appear in this chapbook (see pages 8-9; 10-11; 12-13). A further collection, linking the events of the Holocaust to Jewish history, appeared in 1949. Sachs, who was stateless, having had her German citizenship revoked in 1941 because she was Jewish, was granted Swedish citizenship in 1952. She published a new collection of her own poetry every few years, as well as several translations of Swedish poets. But she remained relatively unknown in the Federal Republic of Germany at this time. From the first years in Sweden she had begun to read more extensively, especially the works of Jewish scholars such as Gershom Scholem and Martin Buber. Probably from Scholem she took her interest in the Kabbalah, the Jewish mystical tradition which had begun to be formulated in Southern Europe in the late twelfth century, and is often seen to have a universalising aspect. This latter aspect was of particular interest to Sachs, who was familiar with Christian teaching, and many images from Jewish and Christian religious thought appear in her writing.

Though Sachs was by nature a retiring person, she formed many friendships with Swedish and German writers, as well as those from other areas of Europe, like Paul Celan, during the 1950s, and throughout all this time she continued to study works of history, philosophy and religion, reading Danish philosopher Søren Kierkegaard, French philosopher and mystic Simone Weil, and many others. In 1958, she got to know German poet Hans Magnus Enzensberger, who became editor for the Suhrkamp publishing house in 1960, one of the major West German publishers of German literature. Enzensberger and Suhrkamp were instrumental in ensuring her work reached a wider audience. Like

Paul Celan, Sachs believed that poetry was a form of communication. From her earliest post-war poems, it is clear that she saw her role as providing a voice for those who had been murdered in the Holocaust, and some of her best early poetry questions the role she has taken on.

In 1961 Enzensberger edited *Fahrt ins Staublose* (Journey to a Dustless Realm). The poems in this collection show that she has now moved from the weighty sense of identification with Jewish suffering to poetry that is sparer in form, more restrained in its expressions of suffering, and that concentrates more on the questions that need to be asked in the aftermath of the Holocaust.

By this time, Sachs had had a number of stays in hospital, necessitated by mental breakdowns, when she would relive the trauma of the fear she and her mother had experienced in Berlin, as well as the death of her mother ten years after their flight. Yet she continued to write poetry as well as plays and essays throughout her illnesses.

Swedish writer and critic, Aris Fioretos, describes how the development away from her earlier, more explicit poems was in part the result of her reading, and in part of her growing confidence as a poet as she interacted more with other poets (Fioretos 2011: 256-8). She was certainly also influenced by her translation work and the familiarity this had given her with other ways of writing. So it is rather unfortunate that Nelly Sachs' best-known (and most anthologised) poems in English translation tend to be the early ones, where there is explicit Holocaust imagery: chimneys, ashes, smoke. The later, sparer and more complex poems have often been avoided as difficult or mysterious. Her collection *Glühende Rätsel* (Glowing Enigmas), first published in four parts from 1964 to 1966, and translated by Michael Hamburger, is indeed not easy to understand without context, and the publication of the complete English version in one volume in 2011 is unlikely to have gained her new readers, in spite of the excellence of the translation.

From the mid-1960s on, as Sachs became more famous, she was awarded a number of prizes, including the *Friedenspreis des Deutschen Buchhandels* (German Publishing Peace Prize) in 1965 and the Nobel Prize, which she received the following year on her seventy-fifth birthday. Yet she was still misunderstood – and often described after her Nobel Prize award – as the poet of reconciliation and healing. This seems wrong. It is not that she was not in favour of reconciliation, since she often expressed her view that it was essential, but that this is not all she said, by any means. In her poetry she is often ironical, despairing, questioning, fearful.

A great deal has been written about Nelly Sachs, and her name is famous around the world, but her work appears not to be very much read. Because of the complexity of her later poetry, she is often regarded as a difficult poet, and Enzensberger's comment, introducing the 1967 *Selected Poems*, with translations by Michael Hamburger, Ruth Mead, Matthew Mead, and others, that her work is "great and mysterious", probably did not help (Sachs 1967: v). Swedish writer Bengt Holmqvist, in his introduction to the 1968 *Das Buch der Nelly Sachs* (The Book of Nelly Sachs), a selection of poems of the 40s, 50s and 60s, with several essays on Sachs' work, describes her language overall as that of "Sehnsucht" (longing; Holmqvist 1968: 9). Her biographer, Gabriele Fritsch-Vivié, speaks of "despair, especially in the later work" (Fritsch-Vivié 1993: 135). Her longing was in part for union with God, in part for an understanding of the relationship between God and the word, and of her own role in that relationship as someone who worked with words. And she often expressed despair at the very emptiness and incomprehensibility that had always spurred her on to write. As she entered her final years, she suffered from heart problems and cancer. She died in 1970, shortly after hearing of the death of Paul Celan.

REFERENCES

Fioretos, A., *Nelly Sachs, Flight and Metamorphosis: An Illustrated Biography*, translated from the Swedish by T. Tranæus, (Stanford, CA: Stanford University Press, 2011).

Fritsch-Vivié, G., *Nelly Sachs*, (Reinbek: Rowohlt, 1993).

Holmqvist, B. (ed.), *Das Buch der Nelly Sachs*, (Frankfurt am Main: Suhrkamp, 1968).

Sachs, N., *Selected Poems*, translated from the German by M. Hamburger, C. Holme, R. Mead, M. Mead, M. Roloff, (London: Jonathan Cape, 1967).

BIOGRAPHICAL NOTES

Leonie Sachs, always known as Nelly, was born in Berlin in 1891, into a wealthy Jewish family. An only child, close to both parents, Nelly had a sheltered, contented childhood, but suffered a serious mental breakdown in her late teens. She recovered, nursing her father in his final illness, and publishing accomplished but not very original poems in journals and newspapers until the Nazis came to power in 1933. Having spent the next years living in fear for their lives, Sachs and her mother escaped to Sweden in 1940, where Sachs became a translator of modern Swedish poetry into German, continuing to publish her own work, now influenced by the new poetry she had translated, as well as, increasingly, by the events of the Holocaust and her growing understanding of Jewish culture. She became a Swedish citizen in 1952. She suffered several more mental breakdowns, affected by the trauma of her time in Nazi Germany, the fate of the European Jews, and the death of her mother. But she wrote prolifically, and her poetry became very highly regarded in Germany. In 1966 she was awarded the Nobel Prize for Literature. She died in 1970.

Jean Boase-Beier is a translator and editor of poetry, and an academic writer. Her poetry translations include collections, all with Arc Publications, by modern German poets Ernst Meister (2003), Rose Ausländer (2014), Volker von Törne (2017), and Paul Celan (2021), and she co-edited (with Marian de Vooght) *Poetry of the Holocaust: An Anthology* (2019).

Her academic work focuses on translation, style and poetry, and particularly on the translation of Holocaust poetry. Academic publications include *Translating the Poetry of the Holocaust* (2015, Bloomsbury), *Translation and Style* (2020, Routledge) and the co-edited volumes *Translating Holocaust Lives* (2017, Bloomsbury) and *The Palgrave Handbook of Literary Translation* (2018).

Jean is Professor Emerita of Literature and Translation at the University of East Anglia, where she founded the MA in Literary Translation in 1992 and ran it until 2015. She is Arc's Translations Editor.